fanSHEN and Ovalhouse present

Same Same

by
Shireen Mula

Playdead.Famous Publications

Published by Playdead.Famous Publications 2011

© Shireen Mula 2011

Shireen Mula has asserted her rights under the Copyright, Design and Patents Act, 1988, to be identified as the author of this work.

A CIP catalogue record for this book is available from the British Library.

ISBN 978-0-9563749-2-9

Playdead.Famous Publications
www.playdeadfamous.com

Same Same
by Shireen Mula

First produced at Ovalhouse on Tuesday 22 November 2011.

Cast

ASHA	Zoë Nicole
NID	Bharti Patel
RAY	Joseph Radcliffe

Creative team

Directors	Dan Barnard & Rachel Briscoe
Lighting Designer	Michael Nabarro
Composer	Richard Hammarton
Costume Designer	Chris Gylee
Stage Manager	Phillip Richardson

Press	Laura Willis for Thursday's Child
Image	KARBORN

This production has been supported by:

This production also gratefully acknowledges the support of the Garrick Charitable Trust.

We would like to thank Ola Animashawun, Michael Atavar, Mike Bartlett, Conrad Blakemore, Felicity Davidson, Suzanne Gorman, Vicky Graham, Sharron Hall, Val Hoskins, Mark Inger, Steve King, Nadine Khadr Renton, Ruth Little, Sabrina Mahfouz, Don McCamphill, Indhu Rubasingham, Matthew Scott, Alison Solomon, Nina Steiger, Nic Wass and the staff of Ovalhouse.

Cast

Zoë Nicole – ASHA

Zoë has recently graduated from East 15 Acting School (BA Acting). Credits whilst training include Stacey (*Trolls*), Rosa *(Saturday Sunday Monday)* and Lady Macduff/ First Witch (*Macbeth*). Other credits include Elisha (*Thugz n Tearz/* Edinburgh Fringe) and Laurie (*Mother Told Me/* Golden Delilah) Zoë is also a member of Fragments Theatre company headed by artistic director Shane Dempsey.

Bharti Patel – NID

Hello. Many thanks for coming to see the show. This is my first time at Ovalhouse and it's been a pleasure, so thank you to everyone for making me feel at home. I hail from Coventry and I'm not scared to say it. So, what can I say ... see you in the bar, mine's a lager and let's put the world to rights. If however you're legging it, safe journeys, be warm, be happy and keep smiling.

Joseph Radcliffe – RAY

Joseph Radcliffe trained at Drama Centre London. Theatre includes *Assassins* (Time Warner/Old Vic); *The Family Cookbook* (Salisbury Playhouse/ tour); *Moshing Lying Down* (fanSHEN/ tour); *Seven Other Children* (Bolton Octagon); *Sense* (Southwark Playhouse), 24 Hour Plays - *The Freelancers* (Old Vic). Television includes *The Home Office Show*.

Creative Team

Dan Barnard – Co-director

Dan is artistic director of fanSHEN. For fanSHEN, he has directed *Meetings* by Mustapha Matura (Arcola Theatre) and co-directed *Shooting Rats* by Peter Turrini (Lilian Baylis site); *Moshing Lying Down* by Marcelo dos Santos (Shunt, PULSE, festivals tour); *Blowing* by Jeroen van den Berg (national tour); and *Fixer* by Lydia Adetunji (Ovalhouse). His freelance directing work includes *Three Way* by Yusra Warsama (Birmingham Rep); *Colors* by Peca Stefan (Tristan Bates) and *Begin Again* by Elinor Cook (Old Vic New Voices 24 Hour Plays). Dan's work as assistant director includes *Jerusalem*, directed by Ian Rickson; *Oedipus the King* (Cambridge Arts Theatre), directed by Annie Castledine and *A Dulditch Angel* (Eastern Angles Tour), directed by Orla O'Loughlin. Dan was a runner up for the Jerwood Award and the JMK Award in 2008.

Rachel Briscoe – Co-director/ Producer

Rachel is creative director of fanSHEN. For fanSHEN, she has co-directed *Fixer* (Ovalhouse); *Blowing* (national tour); *Moshing Lying Down* (Shunt, PULSE, festivals tour) and *Shooting Rats* (Lilian Baylis site), and directed *Full Circle* (Ovalhouse). Freelance directing includes *Colors* by Peca Stefan (Tristan Bates Theatre); *Inches Apart* (Winner of the Old Vic New Voices Theatre 503 Award); *As Vingadoras* (a clown version of The Avengers with Galician company Maquinaria Pesada). Rachel has assisted on shows by Tiata Fahodzi and Talawa, and is a member of the Old Vic New Voices Club. As a writer, Rachel has trained at the Royal Court and Soho Theatre; her play *Under Racehorses* received a rehearsed reading at Soho and she wrote fanSHEN's adaptation of *Shooting Rats*. Rachel is training as a Feldenkrais practitioner and also works as Director of Theatre at Ovalhouse.

Chris Gylee – Costume Designer

For fanSHEN: *Fixer, Shooting Rats*.

Chris trained at Bristol Old Vic Theatre School and was a selected designer on Cheek by Jowl's inaugural Young Director/Designer programme. For Shakespeare at the Tobacco Factory, he has designed *Hamlet, The Taming of the Shrew, Othello and Much Ado About Nothing*. Other plays include *Henry V* (Southwark Playhouse); *Colörs* and *Tattoo* (Company of Angels); *Grimms - The Final Chapter* (Trafalgar Studios); *Not Knowing Who We Are* (The Blue Elephant) and designs for Arts Ed, Theatre 503, Bristol Old Vic, and The Jermyn Street Theatre. Site-specific designs: *Fanshen* (Theatre Delicatessen); *Oliver Twist* (the egg). Chris is an associate designer with Fairground for whom he designed *The Red Man, Out of Touch* and *Bonnie & Clyde*. Chris's work as an illustrator and artist includes performance collaborations with Bristol Ferment.

Richard Hammarton – Composer

For fanSHEN: *Fixer, Blowing, Shooting Rats*.

Other theatre includes *Edward II, Dr Faustus* (Manchester Royal Exchange); *Speaking in Tongues* (Duke of Yorks); *Ghosts* (The Duchess); *Persuasion, People at Sea, The Real Thing, Arsenic and Old Lace, Les Liasions Dangereuses* (Salisbury Playhouse); *Pride and Prejudice* (Bath Theatre Royal and National Tour); *The Mountaintop* (Trafalgar 1/ Theatre 503); *Breakfast With Mugabe* (Bath Ustinov); *Some Kind of Bliss, World's End, Hello and Goodbye* (Trafalgar Studios); *The Rise and Fall of Little Voice* (Harrogate); *A Raisin in the Sun, Six Characters Looking for an Author* (Young Vic); *Dealers Choice, The Shooky* (Birmingham Rep); *The Lifesavers* (Theatre 503/ Colchester Mercury); *Ship of Fools, Salt Meets Wound, Inches Apart* (Theatre 503). TV/Film Composition includes: *Agatha Christie's Marple* (Series 3, 4 and The Secret of Chimneys, ITV); *Wipeout* (Children's Drama); *Sex 'n' Death* (BBC). TV/Film Orchestration includes *Primeval, Jericho, Agatha Christie's Marple (series 1 & 2); If I Had You,*

Take Me (ITV); *Dracula, Silent Witness, The Ship* (BBC); *Alice Through The Looking Glass* (Ch4).

Shireen Mula – Writer

Shireen's work has been performed in traditional venues including Soho Theatre and Hampstead Theatre as well as site-specifically on the London Underground and in Greenwich Park. She has been on attachment with the Royal Court Theatre, Tamasha Theatre Company, Firehouse Creative Productions USA as well as Nottle Theatre in South Korea where her play *Dog* was translated into Korean. Shireen founded and facilitates *20/20* a new writing course for writers with disabilities at Blue Elephant Theatre. Her work for young people includes *Nameless,* Travelling Light Theatre Company and *Portsmouth,* Blue Elephant Theatre. She is an Associate Artist at Soho Theatre and is currently under commission by Emergency Exit Arts. Shireen is half-Irish and half-Mauritian but her childhood was spent in Saudi Arabia.

Michael Nabarro – Lighting Designer

For fanSHEN: *Shooting Rats*

Michael's recent lighting designs include *The 14th Tale* (Cottesloe Theatre & touring); *Untitled* (Bristol Old Vic, Soho Theatre & touring); *The World's Wife* (Trafalgar Studios & touring); *Ghosts in the Gallery* (Polka Theatre); *Coming Home, The Ballad of Crazy Paola, The Lady from the Sea, An Enemy of the People* & *The Blind* (Arcola Theatre); *Our Share of Tomorrow, Lough/Rain, Limbo* & *1984* (York Theatre Royal); *Slaves, Beasts & Cocoa* (Theatre 503). Michael is a graduate of the RADA Lighting Design course. He previously graduated from Cambridge University and spent three years managing the ADC Theatre in Cambridge.

Phillip Richardson – Stage Manager

As Stage Manager: *66 Books* (Bush Theatre); *Tonight Sandy Grierson will Lecture, Dance and Box* (Edinburgh Festival 2011); *Theatre Brothel* (UK Tour); *Landscape and Monologue* (Ustinov Studio, Bath); *Stuck in the Throat* (Hen and Chickens Theatre / Exeter Fringe Festival); *So On And So Forth* (Accidental Festival, Edinburgh festival 2011); *The York Realist* (Riverside Studios); *State Fair; Generous* (Finborough Theatre); *Olive Juice* (Lion and Unicorn Theatre); *The Collector* (Etcetera Theatre); *Oleanna* (The Carriageworks, Leeds). As Production Manager: SUBS; *Pay As You Go, Hotel Sorrento, Edward Bond Season, Pins and Needles* (Cock Tavern Theatre); *Peter Gill season* (Riverside Studios).

fanSHEN tells stories of real people exploring big questions.
We seek to challenge, confound and surprise.

fanSHEN's work is built on five core elements:

STORY: the aesthetic of each production grows from the story
at its heart. In our work, each element of the story is told by the
theatrical tool that can articulate it best.

LOCAL: fanSHEN's shows are specific to a place, a point in time
and a group of people. They are inspired by the encounters we
see, the sounds we hear, and the way people relate to the
space they are in.

INTERNATIONAL: fanSHEN creates productions in dialogue with
international traditions of theatre which value the visual
alongside the spoken.

DUAL PERSPECTIVE: our work is co-directed, enabling us to
combine the psychological and behavioural detail of a
character-led approach with the aesthetic coherence of an
audience-led approach.

COLLABORATION: we work closely with professionals and
communities, especially young people, to develop work with
relevance and appeal. Dialogue is at the heart of fanSHEN's
artistic practice and collaborators are welcomed into a team
with the co-directors at its centre.

fanSHEN was founded in 2005 by Dan Barnard and Rachel Briscoe. Our associate designer is Chris Gylee and we have a group of associate artists with whom we train and collaborate regularly. In 2010 fanSHEN were awarded the Young Angels Theatremakers Award; in 2011, Dan and Rachel were nominated for the Off West-End 'Best Director' Award for *Fixer*.

In 2012, fanSHEN will make *Green and Pleasant Land*, a pedal-powered outdoor show about Englishness and sustainability.

fanshen.org.uk
@fanshentheatre

Anti-heroes and underdogs.
Stories told sideways.
The things under the bed.
Theatre for people with something to say.
New work for new audiences.

OVALHOUSE

Since the 1960s, Ovalhouse has been a pioneering supporter of queer, feminist and diverse performance work. We remain committed to challenging preconceptions of what theatre is and can be.

Ovalhouse's current programme embodies our commitment to true artistic diversity, our appetite for experimentation with form and our dedication to process.
ovalhouse.com | @ovalhouse

Autumn 2011 – Lady-Led

Lady-Led is an invitation to re-examine how gender functions as an element of artistic practice. Simply, it means that the lead artist on each project in the season is female – but the work is definitely not about 'women's issues'. The title Lady-Led itself implies a neatness, a conformity that the work explodes. This is a season by artists defining their own terms. It exists in dialogue with the idea of what a lady is, looks like, behaves like, makes work about. Gender is the context, the relevant constraint of the situation, the outside edges. We invite you to experience what is happening in the space between.

Lagan by Stacey Gregg | 26 Oct – 12 Nov
Tomboy Blues by Mars.tarrab | 1 – 19 Nov
TaniwhaThames by Stella Duffy & Shaky Isles | 15 Nov – 3 Dec
Same Same by Shireen Mula | 22 Nov – 10 Dec

Lambeth Arts

ARTS COUNCIL ENGLAND

Same Same

For Marlise,

I hope you found what you were looking for.

CHARACTERS:

NID (pronounced "need") – female, 42 years old, first generation British-Indian
ASHA – female, 21 years old, mixed race: White-Asian
RAY – male, 24 years old

NOTE: A "/" in the text indicates where an overlap begins.

This text went to print before the end of rehearsals and so may differ slightly from the play as performed.

NID- He hands me; me – covered in blood, me – coated in pieces of us, he hands me to her.
Her – covered in sweat.
Her – face smothered with hair.
Scream, cry, suck the air in – my first breath.
He looks at the clock - 7:35a.m.
She coos, pushes the hair from her eyes – shhh baba my baba hello, welcome, good morning, hello.
My first everything.
She holds me tight to her breast – warm, warm, scared, comforted – a web.
Her hands, her nails – so big!
I will remember you.
I am born.

ASHA- I'm 1. Mornin' says the calf to the risin' sun. It's 8a.m. I finger the air. Eyes bright - watch ceilin' and clouds and twinklin' light. I'm awake for hours, days maybe. Layers of soft brushed cotton freckle my body.
Bear? Bear with eyes black as ink, where are you? Bear who holds my hand, who tells me good mornin' and kisses good night? Where are you? Close my eyes and see him bury his face into a cloud.
Goodnight Bear – convince myself Bear will return with the next sun.

NID- Just after 8 in the morning.
Bang my spoon against the table, kick my legs out far and push a cube of mango between my teeth.

Adnan – racing his car against his digger across - ni naw ni naw! Brrrrr brrrrr CRASH!
Mum – mashing up sardines for Dad's sandwiches.
Dad – round, blocky, small.
Me – finished!
Nid, never waste food.
He pushes the bowl back towards me.
Chillie – I demand.
Like father like daughter - he smiles as he drizzles chillie over the fruit.
One for Nid, one for Dad, one for Nid, one for Dad.
Cars and diggers, planes and trains deliver food to my mouth and together we finish. Together.
I am 2.

ASHA- I'm 3.
There's a man.
Shoulders far apart.
Chin down.
Infiltratin' gaze. Bullets.
Bastard.
Back of the hand kind of a bastard.
Back of the hand if she was lucky, front of the foot if not.
Bundles me. Bundles of me - eye pokin' out here, ear there, a toe on the left. Carries me, heaves me, heaves all of us – me, sheets, clothes, bread, bananas, a blade, slippers on her feet – she heaves all of us outta his back of the hand kind of a house, blood still tacky 'bove her eyebrow.

In my head I hear him snore. Still.
9:18 a.m.
I've got her, that's all that matters.

NID- 10:34a.m., Adnan and I under the table.
Boiled egg in one hand.
Spoon in the other.
Eating it fast but careful. So careful.
All scooped out? Check, check...
Missed a bit, eat it!
K.
Good.
K.
Quick, quick! He's coming! Go stupid, hurry!
We - climb up to the table. Find the egg cup and
place the empty egg back into it, but this time it's
upside down – looks flawless!
Check, check, good?
Yeah.
Perfect.
Lick the spoon clean, rest it by the egg and dive
under the table again.
Shhh shhh, giggling, shhhh! Hide!
Slipper's on the carpet.
Slipper's pulling out the chair.
Slipper's taking spoon in his hand.
Shhh, shhh.
Slipper's slapping the spoon against the egg's smooth
shell.

Hands can't hold it in anymore! Roll over onto our
backs with laughter.
Slipper's head peers under the table.
He – face grinning, empty egg in hand.
We, together, we snort and tumble.
I am 4.

ASHA- I'm 5, it's 11:09a.m.
What's your name Little Girl?
Who's he callin' Little Girl, I can read!
Gina. What's your name Little Boy?
Elliot. You got any brothers or sisters?
No.
I've got a big brother. Who's that?
My mum.
She doesn't look like you.
Yes she does.
Doesn't.
Does.
Doesn't.
Does.
Doesn't doesn't doesn't.
Take a handful of sand from the pit, shove it up his
mouth and in his nose and –
DOES DOES DOES -
See a boy, an older, bigger boy, boy that looks like
Elliot. He begins to move towards us.
Run to mum. Run. Take her deep brown hand in
mine -

Can I have a brother? A sister? I need one. Just one.
Need someone the same. For me. To protect me. I'll
protect him too.
Please?
I don't want to be the only one.

NID- It's 11:43a.m.
Have you just come back from holiday?
No.
Look like you have.
Do I? I've never been anywhere.
I've been to Spain.
Wow.
Swam in the sea, with fishes.
Lucky.
Yeah.
I am 6.

ASHA- It's 1:20 in the afternoon.
Bread.
Apples.
Book.
2 felt tip pens – green, yellow.
Pencil.
Paper.
Bear.
Pillow.
£6.42 – 1 five pound note, 1 pound coin, 1 twenty
piece, 1 ten piece, 4 two penny pieces, 4 pennies.
Tissues.

Bar of soap.
Hair brush.
Tooth brush.
2 pairs underwear.
2 pairs socks.
Plastic bag.
I draw a picture. Me. Me with a line drawn down me,
right down my face down my nose, down my middle.
I tear along this line – tear me in two. I put the right
away – into my bag. I hold onto the left, I'm going to
hold it all day.
Tomorrow I'm going to try again but I'll hold onto the
right instead. See if that works.
I've been gone for 2 days.
They still haven't found me.
I'm 7.

NID- I am 8.
I'm wearing Adnan's jeans and his blue t-shirt, one
that says 'Robot'. He's in my pink and white dress,
short sleeves, knee-length skirt. Tight on him -
Fat! Piggie, piggie!
Bury under the covers.
Get the torch!
Warm, sheltered, safe here, happy here, watch the
blue light against the white sheets.
Now - bouncing on his bed
Oink! Oink! Piggie, piggie, oink!
Bounce.
Laugh.

Bounce.
Laugh.
Bounce -
Grab scissors from his pencil case.
Green scissors.
Thick plastic handle.
Cut a chunk from my hair.
Laughing.
Almost screaming with the
side splitting
pure
unadulterated
laughter.
Together we wrap my brown hair around the scissors
and cut. Together we cut and watch the threads
settle on the sheet.
Slipper's at the door.
Laughing, crying laughing, want him to join in, we
want –
He - ripping us apart.
He - ripping my dress off Adnan.
Crying, screaming but not from the laughter.
It's July, afternoon, 2:00p.m.
You will wear a hat NID. For the rest of the summer
NID. For the rest. Adnan you are no longer friends
with Richard, no more, enough.

ASHA- I'm 9, in a shoppin' centre, not sure which.
There's a man.
There's a man.

There's a woman.
I can't find.
Where's...
I'm lost.
Is that -?
No.
A long skirt. Black with small small white flowers.
No.
Cling to her leg.
Cling to his leg.
Faces lookin' down at my face.
Not the face I wanna see.
Where's the face? Where're the blue-grey eyes?
Where's –
There's a man.
There's a woman.
There's a woman.
Want to ask a question.
Can I ask a question?
Where's –
Where's –
I'm scared.
Want someone bigger - someone grown, they'll
know.
But I can't see anyone like that, no one that looks like
they'll know the answer; know how, where, what.
Said she'd be 3 minutes, said sit here 3 minutes. Look
at the clock – little hand near the 3, big hand was on
the 1 before, now it's on the 10...
Where's –

Telephone rings and rings, rings out

NID- I am 10.
We're at Naani's house.
Mum rocks me in her lap.
My knees pulled up and in, her arms round me, the whole of me – this is our shape.
I'm bored.
Shhhh baba, shhh.
But I don't understand.
I know, I know.
I want to go home.
Don't say that.
Why not?
You're being rude.
She doesn't even understand.
You are still being rude.
Why can't she just learn English?
She's old now.
We live in England.
She can't change. Listen.
No.
Listen, you'll learn to understand.
I don't want to. Shouldn't have to – we're English.
Nid…
Can we go home yet?
10 more minutes, at 20 past 3, ok?
Ok.

I snuggle close to her, remembering – warmth, fear, comfort.

ASHA- I'm 11, I don't wanna go, don't wanna. I won't. Won't. Let go o' my arm. Go. Please. Hurtin' me, you're -
There's a car - blue Toyota.
There's a car and they're pullin' me, pushin' me – No!
She needs me, she needs, I need her, please. Please.
They – best for you, what's best for you, for you...
I – please, please, she's what's best for me.
My mum – been there all my life.
My house – been there all my life.
They're my home!
I - I'm sorry. I'm sorry.
I've done somethin' bad, very bad. Must have. Don't remember, don't know wha' but, I know now I must have... all this - I must have done something so so wrong for this -
I – take me back!
Forgive me.
Take me back.
When you take me back, only then will I know I've done enough, paid enough.
Then I can stop.
It's 3:57p.m.

NID- I am 12.
Did you used to ride elephants to school?

What?
Did. You. Used. To. Ride elephants. To. School?
No.
Did you not go to school?
What? Yeah, I've always gone to school.
How?
By car.
Do you have cars?
Yes, do you?
Yeah, course *we* do.
It's 4.15p.m.

ASHA- I'm 13. (*reading*) Happy 13th Birthday silly, fabulous, beautiful, crazy Sorya. All my love, always, Mama. Picked it out of my letterbox at 5:30.

NID- Mum? What age were you when you met Dad?
I was 15.
What age was he?
22.
Did you know you were going to marry him?
Yes.
Mum... I like a boy.
Do you?
Yes.
Who is this boy?
He's from school.
Oh.
He kissed me.
Oh.

I am 14.

Yes, yes I suppose you are.

I - move to her, sit on her lap and we make our shape.

She – kisses my hair.

I – he's my boyfriend I think, maybe.

She – is he a nice boy?

Yeah course. D'you not trust me, my judgement? I am smart you know.

I know.

You were 15.

Hmm you are smart.

Can I invite him for dinner?

I'm not sure.

Cause of Dad?

I'm just not sure how he'll feel about you having a boyfriend Nid, you are very young my baba.

Don't call me that.

What? Baba?

Yes. I'm not a baby.

I know. I know.

I'm old enough.

You'll always be a baby in his eyes.

She – moves her hand over my bare knee.

She – rolls the end of my skirt between her thumb and index.

I – hold her hand in mine.

I – gently twirl her wedding ring round and round.

That'll be yours one day my baba.

Mum, I like him.

What's his name?
James.

BEAT

NID- It's your choice darling one.
6:14pm.

ASHA- The incubator at the hospital.
The bunk bed at the children's home.
The single at the De Souza's.
Jimmy's house.
Aisha's house.
Hostel on Kings.
His bed.
His bed.
His bed.
Bathtub.
Corner of Avarard.
Her bed.
The single at the De Souza's.
Garage.
That's 14 different places.
I hope I'll find the right one soon.
I'm tired in the garage at 7:40pm, in the dark,
listenin' to cars drive past.
I'm 15.

NID- I am 16.
My hair is long and straight.

My eyes are brown and oval.
I'm 5ft 4.
Slim.
I am moving my hand towards the latch on the front
door.
Where are you going?
Out.
Out where?
To Claire's. Staying the night, mum said it was ok.
When will you be back?
I don't know, lunch.
Call me.
Fine.
Adnan brushes past, opens door, exits, I try –
Isn't Claire's mum picking you up?
No, walking.
I'll drop you.
I don't need you to.
I'll drop you.
I can walk.
Let's go. It's late.
It's 8:30. It's not far.
Nid…
I just want to walk, alone, just –
Why?
I just do.
You don't want to go with me, is that it? With your
family? Embarrassed by us now?
My eyes - blurry from the arguments.
My head - full.

My mouth
my heart
my truth - silenced by his love.
Ok Dad, you can drive me, let's go.

ASHA- Paul.
Mark.
Mr. Weaver.
Pia.
Skinhead with the acne-back.
Mr. Clements.
Boy from Inferno.
Hostel bloke.
Navy suit, stripy tie, black pointy toe shoes - swollen
lip an' a badly bruised thigh.
White male.
White female.
Black male.
Black female.
Asian male.
White male.
White male.
A different lover for every year.
I watch the clock hit 9:45pm as he pushes my arms
behind my head.
He – what's your name?
I – dunno, and pull him inside of me.
My mind goes blank and there's nothing else –
thoughts, fears, questions, blame.
Thank you.

I'm 17.

NID- I am 18.
I walk.
I walk.
Saturday night - 10:55pm.
Boys and girls scurry.
Boys and girls kiss.
Me – skirt, heels and a backpack.
Backpack full of jeans, flats and make-up remover.
One foot in front of the other and try to keep upright and walking straight.
Yes.
Nearly home now.
Nearly.
Get there before 11, must.
Step 1 – Wiping the make-up off my face now.
Step 2 – Crouching in the dark round the corner from my house and pulling my jeans up and on under my skirt. Begin to pull my skirt down –
Shit - voices.
Shit, shit.
Step 3 – Sprinting, sprinting to my front door, keys keys find my keys, where are–
Hear the word
Paki
Paki
Paki
Paki
Paki

Key in the door.
Twist.
Paki
Paki
Paki
Twist
Please twist!
Twist!
Twists and I'm in.
Rest my back against the door.
Heart in my throat.
Skirt half up half down.
Heels on my feet.
Red face.
Alcohol breath.
He's there.
He sees heels.
He sees face.
He has seen.
Where have you been?
Walk away, I walk away.
Up the stairs.
Into the bathroom.
Lie down on the tiles.
Can hardly hear his words.
Paki paki paki paki.
Knocking.
Banging.
NID.
NID.

Open the door.
Don't.
Won't.
Never heard him this angry before.
Paki paki paki paki.
Feel the cold tiles on my face and block out the din.

ASHA- I'm 19. He's pushin' my arms behind my head.
He's pullin' my top up.
He is sweet and smooth and gentle – he's perfect.
I'm laughin' - laughin' to try to calm my nerves.
I'm hesitatin'.
Why? What's wrong with me?
I'm 19, he's perfect, I'm -
I'm inchin' away.
Fuck.
I've never had sex – the words are out before I can
censor myself.
Fuck.
I've never had sex with anyone, I've never wanted to,
I've never understood it.
I'm a child, sex is adult - that's what adults do, they
make babies.
I -
I'm not an adult.
I can't.
I just -
I'm pullin' my top back on, my jacket – I wish for
more layers.

I'm runnin' from his room, runnin', runnin' from this perfection.
Keep movin' keep going keep –
Never stop never stay
Keep
Run
Go
Go
11pm.
Don't stop

NID- 11pm. I am 20.

Simultaneously ASHA counts quietly but vehemently while NID speaks

ASHA- 20 /19 18 17 16 15 14 13 12 11 10 9 8 7 6 5 4 3 2 3 4 5 6 7 8 9 10 11 12 13 14 15 16 17 18 19 20 19 18 17 16 15 14 13 12 11 10 9 8 7 6 5 4 3 2 3 4 5 6 7 8 9 10 11 12 13 14 15 16 17 18 19 20 19 18 17 16 15 14 13 12 11

NID- He's taking my hand in his own.
He's telling me I'm beautiful.
I can't stop laughing, cannot stop laughing.
I don't believe you.
You are.
Liar.
Believe me!
No!

I wish you would, could.

Beauty, beauty just isn't something I think about.

Why not?

I just don't think about it, don't think about myself like that.

Like what? Like a woman, like a beautiful woman?

I don't even know this man – don't, don't look at me like that. Don't.

I – I don't even know you.

He – yes you do. No one's ever told you that you were beautiful before have they?

I – yes, course they have – that's a lie.

He – I have such an amazing time when I'm with you.

Do you?

Yes. Don't you?

Yes, no, yes I do.

Good. Come see my flat?

No, I mean... I'd like to but I need to get home. It's getting late.

Are you tired?

No.

Then...?

I just, I just can't. Sorry. You're... listen... believe me, I very much very much would like to, ok? Believe me.

I believe you.

I just, I can't, sorry.

It's ok. You're very serious, aren't you?

No. Sometimes. Maybe.

Things weigh heavy on your shoulders.

I don't know how to reply to that.

I –
I –
He – leans into me.
He smells like shampoo - clean and fresh as a
winter's night.
He – moves the back of his hand along my jaw line –
from my ear to the tip of my chin.
He – kisses the side of my mouth.
I – forget time
Forget dates, numbers, night and day.
Forget them.
Take him and I and this moment for me, me alone.
Mine.

.

Let's go to your flat.

.

I'm 20. I forsake everything.
Anything.
More.

ASHA- 10

NID- 10

ASHA- /9

NID- 9

ASHA- 8

NID-/8

ASHA- 7

NID- 7

ASHA- 6

NID- /6

ASHA- 5

NID- /5

ASHA- 4

NID- 4

ASHA- /3

NID- 3

ASHA- /2
Will everything still be the same?

NID- 2
And nothing is the same.

ASHA- 5 to midnight, 1st July.
5 minutes /more…

NID- 300 seconds until -
I was 21.

ASHA- 2nd July – my birthday.

NID- 2nd July – she'll be 21.

ASHA- She's got brown eyes. Dark.

NID- She looks like me.

ASHA- Her eyes are green.

NID- She looks nothing, nothing like me.
Her eyes are -

ASHA- My eyes are hazel.

NID- I was 21.

ASHA- My eyes are /hazel.

NID- I don't remember.

ASHA- Remember. Remember. /Remember

NID- I don't. Don't. /I...

ASHA- I am born.

I'm born fat and round and bouncin' and announcin'
my arrival with roars. I'm passed between bodies like
the best of all presents.
I am born.
I'm born through a slit in her stomach.
Momma's body is still warm.
Her soul departed 3 minutes ago.
In my birth I take her life; my first breath signals her
last.
I'm selfish.
I am born.
I'm born but I don't know if you can call it born.
Can you call it born if you're already dead?
I am born.
I'm born, I have a mother and we've all never been
happier.
17:13, 2nd July 1989
8 pounds, 3 ounces
Mother – Samia Singh
Father – Tony Evans

NID- 1. The Mutton:
Add the marinated mutton, 1 teaspoon garam
masala and salt to taste. Then keep frying until oil
separates from masala.
2. Again heat 1 tablespoon oil and fry whole cloves
and cinnamon sticks. Add rice and fry a little then
add enough hot water and salt to taste. Cook 'til rice
is done.
3. Dissolve saffron in warm milk and keep aside.

4. Take a heavy bottomed pan lined with ghee.
Spread bay leaves at the bottom. Spread a layer of
rice and cover it with half of mutton. Sprinkling half
of dhania, fried onions and one lime juice.
5. Cover with rice followed by a mutton layer and do
the same as before. Finish with a rice layer and
sprinkling the saffron milk. Cover and seal with
aluminum foil. Cook in a preheated oven for 20
minutes. Garnish with egg cut into pieces. Serve hot.
Her favourite for her birthday.
Perfect.

ASHA- 17:13, 2nd July 1989
8 pounds, 3 ounces
Mother – Niamh Byrne
Father – Javad Shah

NID- God, they do grow up fast. Ridiculously.
Absolutely, absolutely ridiculously fast. She lives in
London with some uni friends. Mm. She studies
accounting. Never understood numbers that much,
myself, never, all that... very intelligent, lacks a bit of
common sense sometimes, always think common
sense is more important myself, just my opinion, but
she'll find her way. Have to let them, don't you?
Mmm. She'll be coming to see us tomorrow.
(*calling*) 3, was it 3?
Deaf as a dormouse that one. It was 3.
Roast. She'd like that I think. Lose track don't you -
she hated prawns, when she was a child, mm hated

them, hated their faces, their little bodies, couldn't
look at their little bodies she said. Don't know.
Don't know now.
Maybe she loves them now.
Roast is safe though, isn't it? Chicken. Bit of veg.
Mmm.
Oh the present. Looked for hours, didn't we. We did.
That's what'll happen when you don't know what
you're looking for.
It's a necklace.
Silver and quartzes.
Does that sound...?
Her da though, he loves her, loves her stubbornness
God forgive him. He's so proud, you know. Ah but
he's a good man, Javad, he is. Never left her wanting
for anything, no.
I have lost my temper with her though.
Nothing I'm proud of.
No.
He – patience of a saint. Truly. A good man.

ASHA- 17:13, 2nd July /1989

NID- I've kept the receipt. Just in case.

ASHA- 17:13, 2nd July 1989
8 pounds, 3 ounces
Mother – Maria Henderson
NID- Been here since Tuesday.
Tomorrow's Sunday, think.

Left the house for 10 minutes. Went down
Somerfields. 10 bloody minutes, eh? Can't be. It was
10 minutes...
Bastard.
Cunt.
Milk's gone off now and all.
Don't even want to go into the shower.
Wouldn't hear it then, would I? Nah.
Fuckin' –
Is tomorrow Sunday?
No right.
My name is Maria Henderson - I am worth everythin'
he fuckin' is.
That's what they teach us, in't it?
But here I am.
Not a cup of tea to my name.
Should never have gone out, should never have.
Stupid.
Stupid cunt.
Typical - you go out for 10 minutes and that's when
he chooses to call.
I don't even know.
He didn't call, did he?
Or did I miss the call?
I could have - that 10 minutes...
He could have.
It'd be typical wouldn't it?
Not typical, fuckin' unlikely.
That's his game in't it?

Keep me here, keep me lookin' smellin' like shit so
no one else wants me.
I know his game but every time… we have a cup of
tea, have a sit down…
Don't look into his eyes, don't look, don't –
Can never help myself.
Look into them fuckin' eyes and he can have me then
and there. Have me anyway he wants. Like a fuckin'
dog I am. That's what he says. True and all.
He'll be callin' soon.
Never goes a week.
He never goes a week without me. It hasn't been a
week, has it? No.
He couldn't.
He'd die.
We both would.
Half of the same whole we are.
We are.

Knocking

ASHA- Brought you some milk, carton of soup.

NID- Lovely. Thanks chicken.

ASHA- I took your washin' off the line.

NID- Did you?

ASHA- It was rainin'.

NID- What would I do without you?

ASHA- Be lost?
Be alone?
Broken.
Scared.
Dead.

NID- You didn't see him on your way, no?

ASHA- No.
Would you ever want 'nother?

NID- 'Nother man?

ASHA- 'Nother me.

NID- Never be another you.

ASHA- Thank you.

NID- Couldn't. Broke now. Down there. After you.
Broke.

ASHA- Oh.

NID- Nothin' there now.
Nothin' worth nothin'.

ASHA- I am born.
I'm born without a mum or a dad because they're young, /very young.

NID dials and a phone rings

ASHA- They don't know how to –
They don't know –
I understand that.
They're only 13.

NID- Hello, I'm calling regarding, I'm calling, sorry, I'm...

ASHA- I am born.
I'm born without a mum or a dad because I am the result of violence and pain.
I can understand.
I am unwanted.
I'm half of a man she hates, half of a, a, a, an experience she hates, half of something she wishes to forget.
I can understand.

NID- Hello, I'm calling regarding a child.
A girl.
I don't –
She was born 2nd July 1989.
I don't -

ASHA- I am born.

I'm born without a mum or a dad because there's been an accident.

A car -

Now - sheet of white over her body.

Now - table of white beneath her.

Stirrups hold her open, wide.

Face droopin'.

Eyes shut.

Nothin there.

Man in white mask.

Man in white gloves.

He's pullin', pullin', pullin' out slime 'n' mud 'n' flesh – me.

No pushin' - dead.

At least I came out cryin', wantin' to die with her, cryin' yellin' screamin' at him to leave me be, leave me inside a her, clawin' at her insides, tryna pull myself up in, nowhere else to go.

Please.

Leave me die inside o' her. Let us rot together mould, melt into one, we're half of the same whole we are.

Early I learn that I'm ugly and evil, that I'm to be hated.

I agree.

Understand.

Know.

NID- Hello, I'm calling regarding a girl.

She was born 2nd July 1989.

King's Cross St. Pancras Station, the toilets.

ASHA- I am born.
I'm born without a mum or a dad because they made a decision.
They thought they could, they so badly wanted to but... they couldn't.
They're hardly able to take care for themselves let alone a child.
Me.
They knew this when they held me - so small, so vulnerable - just like them.
So they hand me over gently.
He puts his arm around her shoulders as the services take me away.
They want what's best for me.
They did the best they knew how.
It wasn't their fault.
It's understandable really.
Better.
Best.
Really.

NID- Hello? Hello? Hello!
I'm calling regarding my daughter, born 2nd July 1989.
She was left in London, King's Cross St. Pancras Station in the toilets. She's mixed-race, Asian-white.
Is this who I need to...
Ok. I will.

Thank you.
Thank you.
I'll wait.

.

.

.

My arm was around his when I woke up this morning.
Thick black hair of his arms, his chest, his head and back and everywhere - he's my Bear. I breathed in that moment, a beam of new light bringing my mother's wedding ring to life on my finger 'til the alarm clock screeches then he yawns and stretches, presses the clock between his hands and sinks back into me. I like his weigh, his drowsy warmth. It's morning, even his feet are warm now.
Then small creak.
Small feet.
Small jump and tumble and she's with us.
She's under my arm.
She's soft hair and long eye lashes.
She whispers good morning and we are one, two, three – tiny one, my two and Bear three.
A web - all arm in arm all back to front to back – my family.
Again the alarm and our three is broken, he is up and he is scooping her from our white sheets.
Breakfast, breakfast is toast and orange juice and snap, crackle and pop – the chocolaty kind.

She's talking to the pops, telling them about what
Graham said to Tasha and Lucy said to her and how
she wants to build a tree-house with no ladder and
climb up there every day – all this chatter chatter
from this tiny mouth. All this life from inside of me.
Staring at her, my arm finds his waist and he knows
what I'm thinking, knows what I'm saying though my
lips never moved.

Then she's up, she's standing on her chair – all three
foot of her in powder pink. She's turning the
calendar page over. A new fluffy yellow Labrador
smiles back at us. My daughter's giggling and
whispering – she's a can of coca-cola quivering after
you give it a shake.

Her father is by her side now and they're pinch
punch, pinch punching around our pine table.

This is our ritual for the first of the -

The fluffy Labrador barks.

The dog begins to scratch.

The golden Labrador is now greyish, brownish, not
even a Labrador, not even -

The mongrel is scratching it's way through the pages,
it's -

1st July.

This.

1st.

July.

2010.

1st.

July.

The barking grows louder. The barking becomes
growling, becomes whimpering becomes the
shouting yelling screaming of the 1st of July. My
fingers grip into the countertop behind.
They dig in.
Hands now red.
Nails now black.
I begin to drool and my eyes melt, melt and drip
down my nose, cheeks, chin – burning a trail as they -
His hand on my hand.

.

Mmm, yeah, I'm fine - I swallow and attempt to
breathe.
Don't look them in the eye, don't, don't –
They leave to get their bags, their keys, jackets, their
-
I vomit.
Vomit in the kitchen sink.
Heave the past, present and future from my core and
stare at it.
It's black.
Streaks of red.
Hair. Clumps of –
Finger nails.
It's… I think it's moving.
I think it's got a pulse. I think it's got a face and
brown-green –
I'm turning on the taps.
Yes, just coming, yes.

I'm watching the colours swirl, merge and spiral
down the drain, I'm chucking water left and right,
I'm-
Yes, coming, yes.

.

I don't remember driving.
I don't remember kissing Sara goodbye.
I don't remember kissing Saj goodbye.
I don't remember dialling the number.
I don't remember coughing and feigning sickness.
I don't know where I parked.
Do I have any shoes on?
Is there anything under my feet?
There's a clock.
A huge clock tick, tocking.
Tick tocking pushing onwards but somehow I'm
standing still or I'm moving back or -
Ghost steps – dead long gone steps walk with me, on
me, over me, treading on me, step, step, together,
step.
1
Remember a different body.
2
Remember a heavy body.
3
Remember a strained back, thick swollen ankles and
thick swollen feet, my huge, tumbling breasts.
Carrying you.
Walking with you.
Step, step, together, step.

Walking in pain with you.

I'm 21.

I'm not supposed to be a mother.

7

8

Pain coursing through all the parts of me, remember

13

14

15

Cannot get to the toilets fast enough

20

Breathe

Breathe

Steady

11

12

Hold onto the numbers, the stable, the here, the
now, the real.

Just

8

8

Doing fine, doing fine.

8

8

9

You will not kill me!

I will not have you kill me.

Ni naw ni naw ARRRGH - a small boy screams. I touch
my stomach, it's flat, it's flat, thank you God. It's ok.
I'm ok. The clock is ticking. I watch a woman with a

buggy hurry past, her feet barely touching the ground.

I don't know how long I've been here. Here with all these people, people walking, people lugging cases, people taking steps, going and coming, here and then gone, leaving their lives, going to their lives, living their -

What am I doing here?

I should be at work, I should go, I should -

The sign.

The little white woman in her triangle dress - the sign, the ladies toilets in Kings Cross Station - she looks the same, standing with green light behind her hailing her existence.

Time hasn't aged her a bit - still smooth and bright.

The door.

I can see fingerprints on its handle.

My, my fingerprints.

I can see a fallen hair.

A lost earring, lost 21 years ago.

Spot of blood.

I'm still here.

The woman on the sign... I think she's grinning, smirking – she remembers my face.

I want to stoop towards the earring but I'm getting in the way - I'm in everyone's way. I want to wipe the blood clean but all these people... I'm caught up in their flow... then my hand is clinging, I'm clinging for support onto the doorway of the toilets...

Through this... on the other side of this door...

I look at my feet and they are walking.
I look at my arm and it is pushing open the white
door. My mind cannot halt this. My body knows and
it takes me there.
Past that white door I see my face in mirrors, in long
mirrors and in short, to the left and to the right, all of
them staring back at me.
In those eyes I see my mother.
In that nose I see my father.
My brother has that chin.
I see my stomach huge and round.
My daughter has those lips.
My left hand, my ring finger – no ring, no wedding,
no -
My hips are turning.
My knees are creaking.
My eyes are glaring – I turn and I look.
Look.
Look.
Look.
That's it.
There it is.
The cubicle.
Both my daughters have those lips.
I'm only 42.
I'm only –
I'm 21.
My feet move me through the cubicle door and my
hand closes and locks it behind me - I lock the door.
Lock and

SCREAM.
SCREAM.
SILENT FUCKING SCREAMS.
SCREAM.
Pulling off shoes and tights and everything down below.
Oh God.
Oh God.
I think there's blood.
Is there supposed to be blood?
There was water, fluid before, clear, but red now, is that...? I don't know I don't know I'm 21 I didn't know, I was 21!

.

1 second -
Its head lies on my chest.
Now I know.
Just a second, a split –
We're not. We're not...
And I know.
Don't know how to, it doesn't even look like me.
Drop it.
Put it aside.
I know.
Don't wanna know.
Don't wanna know no no know if it's breathing or not.
Try to put it down.
I – try to put it down, I saw -
I – don't wanna see.

I – see.

A girl.

Girl – screams.

Girl – screams, yells at me.

Girl – tries to wrap her tiny tiny tiny bloody nails round my finger.

Get off, get off get off.

Asha.

I know her name is Asha, that's her name.

I know that.

Know it, Asha Asha, your name is Asha and you are my daughter, mine, all mine all -

No, no crying. This kid, this thing, she doesn't cry. She's angry. No sadness. No one with working ears could ever describe that as a cry. Yelling blistering screaming at me.

SHUT UP

SHUT UP

Someone come, someone?

What do I do?

I – don't want to touch her.

I – don't know how to touch her.

I –

Someone's coming, someone –

Put her – Asha – down.

Down on dirty tiled floor.

Put her down on shit and piss and sweat and cum.

Back where she came from.

Gone.

Little piece a shit.

Gone.

Little stain.

Gone.

Little nothing.

Nothing of mine.

If he wants her, he can come find her.

Greenish, brownish, murky coloured eyes. Make up your mind eyes, do you want green, green fields and green pastures or brown, brown dirt and dust and yellow heat? I could teach you about the heat but you wouldn't want to know. No. Not you. Why would you? You've got emerald hills and glittering white Christmases.

Go back where you came from.

She is born.

ASHA dials, a phone rings

ASHA- Hi.

I'm lookin', I'm callin' 'cause, I'm… I'm -

Dunno if this is the right number but –

Right ok, I'm callin' because I was fostered. I don't know who my real, my biological mother is and… I'd like to, I wanna find her.

Is this the right –

Ok, so wha', wha'… wha' do I do?

Ok, when?

I'll come, I'll come today, now, yeah I'll come…

Thank you, really thank you, bye.

NID- And, did you say that this is your first child – the doctor asks as Saj holds my hand.

Yes, I mutter, yes.

Oh, really? Because...

And she must have seen the fear in my eyes, seen the complete panic – panic like I'd just seen a ghost because

She stopped.

Because...

Stops.

Really? Because... that's great, really, because that's great.

I sigh cobwebs and sand.

The sigh of 8 years of hiding from him and 21 years of hiding from them. You and them.

Knocking

Knocking

Knock

Hurry up Nid.

Coming I'm coming... as I wrap a length of bandage over and over and round and round my stomach, my breasts – around this thing inside of me, push it in and away.

Hurry!

Coming, just 2 seconds Mum!

How can they not know?

Huge jumper.

Do they really not know?

Ridiculously huge -

Knocking

Breathe in.
Knocking
Knock
Coming, I'm coming!

.

Sorry sorry... have I been here long? Sorry, I didn't
realise, time... I thought, just a few minutes... I...
The voice sounds angry, angry or concerned or, I
don't know.
I get to my feet.
Sorry, I'm just coming, yes.
Unlock the cubicle door and out.
Faces stare at me, me - all tear stained and raw.
The cleaner's lips move but I hear nothing as I float
past.
On the 1st of July 2010 I'm gliding.
Colours and noises all merge into one spinning
throbbing mass around me and somehow I'm on a
platform.
I don't know what platform but I am, I'm on a
platform.
Jessop
Jevons
Jewers
Jewett
Jewitt
Jewkes
Jewson
Jobson
Johannson

John
Johns
Johnson
Johnston
Johnstone
Jolly
Jonas
Jones
Jopson
Jordan
Jordi -
Jordan
Foster Care.
Adopted by Mr. and Mrs. Jordan, Suffolk.
Are you happy?
Are you happy there?
I hope you're happy there.
That's what I wanted.

ASHA- What?

NID- I wanted you to be happy.

ASHA- Who is this?

NID- Your name's Asha.

ASHA- My name's Alex.

NID- You sound ok, you sound good, your accent, it's lovely and, that's, that's what I, that's all I needed to know. Thank you. Thanks for... are you there?

BEAT

NID- Asha?

BEAT

NID- Sorry.
That's the name I wanted for you.
Sorry, I should, I should call you Alex, shouldn't I?

BEAT

NID- Do you want me to stop? Go?

BEAT

NID- Ok.
Good/bye

ASHA- No.

NID- I thought, thought you didn't want me to –

ASHA- I don't know what I want.
I've rehearsed this in my head a thousand times, but now, now it's all...

NID- I know, me too. I could ask you questions? Would that help?

ASHA- Ok.

NID- Do you like where you're living?

ASHA- It's ok, I like it alright.

NID- Good.
And your... the people, the Jordan's, who look after you, they're alright?

ASHA- Yeah, they're fine.

NID- Are you in school?

ASHA- Uni.

NID- Brilliant, what are you –

ASHA- Engineering.

NID- Wow

ASHA- Yeah?

NID- Yeah.

BEAT

NID- Will you, would you meet me?

BEAT

NID- You don't have to, if you don't want to.

ASHA- I'm not sure.

NID- Well just, let me know.

ASHA- How?

NID- Well...

ASHA- What's your phone number?

NID- ...

ASHA- Why did you leave me?

NID- We could talk about this in person, I think, I think it'd be –

ASHA- Why did you leave me?

NID- I'm trying to make up for it now.

ASHA- Do you have any money?

NID- Money?

ASHA- I need, I want some money.

NID- Oh.
Well, how much would you need?

ASHA- Grand, two grand.

NID- £2,000?

ASHA- Yes.

NID- I don't think, I mean, I'm not sure that I –

ASHA- If you'd done your job, if you'd been looking after me for the last 21 years you'd have spent a lot more than that.

NID- Yes.

ASHA- You owe me.

NID- I'll give you a cheque when we meet.

ASHA- Post it.

NID- I –
Ok.

Who should I make it out to?

ASHA- Alex Jordan.

NID- Where d'you live?

ASHA- Why?

NID- To post –

ASHA- I don't want to give you my address.

NID- How can I –

ASHA- I don't want to give you my address.

NID- Ok.
Tell me what you want.

ASHA- Post it to 23 Kenway Road, SE17 8HY.

NID- Is that your address?

ASHA- No.

NID- Whose name shall I write on the envelope?

ASHA- Alex Jordan.

NID- But that's not your address?

ASHA- No.

NID- Ok.
I, shall I give you my phone number, you /could –

ASHA- No.

NID dials, phone rings

ASHA- Hi.

BEAT

ASHA- Can I help you?

NID- I just, are you Marwa?

ASHA- Who's askin?

NID- Just… just me.

ASHA- Right, and who are you?

NID- From the, from the council?

ASHA- What?

NID- About your T.V. license.

ASHA- I don't own a T.V.

NID- Oh.
Did you ever have one?

ASHA- No.

NID- Right, well we need to update our, our records then.

ASHA- Right.

NID- I'm sorry, I'm very sorry to have bothered you.

ASHA- Yeah.

NID- Thank you for your time and for, /for

ASHA- Yeah, bye.

NID dials, phone rings

ASHA- You sound young.

NID- I'm 42.

ASHA- I'm 21.

NID- I know.

ASHA- You left me.

NID- Yes. Abandoned.

ASHA- To die.

NID- Floor. Smell of shit and urine-

ASHA- Hate you.

NID- Me too.

ASHA- Die.

NID- I've tried.

ASHA- Kill you.

NID- Please.

ASHA- What do you want?
Why are you calling me? Why are you doin' this?

NID- I needed to know –

ASHA- YOU NEEDED?

NID- I'm sorry.

ASHA- A baby.

A child.
I NEEDED.

NID- You don't have to see me.

ASHA- I won't.

NID- Don't have to hear from −

ASHA- Not your decision.
Mine.

NID- Yes.

ASHA- You don't get to make -

NID- No.
It's yours.

ASHA- Then no.
No.
Never.
Don't.
Don't.
Ever.

NID- Ok.
Thank you.

ASHA- Force this on me.

Didn't know who was calling. Didn't have the chance-

NID- I'm sorry.
Yes.

ASHA- Not your choice. Not yours.

NID- I'm going to go now.

ASHA- NO.
You stay.

NID- You want me to?
You want to –

ASHA- No.
You stay and you listen to me until I say GO.
I SAY GO.

NID- Ok.

ASHA- You're a bitch.

NID- Yes.

ASHA- Don't speak.
Don't dare interrupt.

BEAT

ASHA- Your voice sounds like finger nails dragging
through gravel.
Fuckin' ugly.
Most.
Most.
Ugly.
Never heard such –
42?
You were 21.
Stupid.
How stupid can you be?
Fuckin' imbecile. Snot faced little -
Your parents musta been ashamed, shame, musta
been disgusted, you doin that, doin' that, probably
been doin' it for years by that time hey? You brown?
You white? Which were you? Fuckin white men to
make yourself feel bigger, better proud or fuckin'
some paki to raise your neighbours' eyebrows? Be
dirty, be a slag, fuckin' slut, fuckin' deviant, fuckin'
freak.

BEAT

NID- You'll always be a part of me.
I'll /always be a part of you.
No matter –

ASHA- No. I made this.
I made me.

I'm done. This is it. And it ain't got nothin' to do with you.

NID- Our blood, /our –

ASHA- Fuck you.
I hope that you can't sleep.
I hope that every one of your waking hours is filled with images of me.
Good bye.

NID- Ash –

DEAD DIAL TONE

ASHA- So how long d'you think...?
.
Just a guess...
.
Wha', wha' weeks? Months? We're not... I mean it's not gonna take longer than that, yeah?
.
Wait, but are there... are there times when you can't, you just can't –
Have there been times you just haven't been able to track them down, ever?
.
But -
You're, you're gonna try?
.

Thank you. Thank you. Bye.

NID- Live with it or die with it…
I'm sorry, I'm sorry you weren't born to someone
else.
Too good for me, you were too good for me anyway.
But
I want you to know something Ash.
I want you to know that I went back.
I left you.
Yes.
I left you in the toilets, in this station.
But I went back.
Keep on going back - in my head, constantly, always,
through it all, I am forever trying to go -
I went back, back, I run back, I run and drip sweat,
run and blood trickles down my thigh, lose an earring
don't care, run, tears, screams…
Girl in the white triangle dress
Arrow
Door
In
Here
But
Empty.
Gone.
You've gone.
You're… you're gone.
Too late.
I went back but you're gone, I'm too late.

Don't know what to do.
Don't know what to –
Can't tell anyone.
Can't ask any one.
There's a man.
A man.
Woman.
I can't find.
Where's…
I'm lost.
Faces looking -
Not the face I wanna see.
Where's the face? Where're the hazel eyes?
Where's –
A man.
There's a woman.
There's a woman.
Want to ask a question, but -
Can I ask a question?
Where's –
Where's –
I'm scared.
Want someone bigger – someone grown, they'll
know.
Have
Have
Have you seen my baby?
Have you -
No. No. Don't ask, can't, no.
Live with it.

Sit with it.
Seep with it.
Die with it.
I'm sorry.
I'm sorry I left you.
I'm sorry you weren't born to someone better than me.
But went back Ash, I went back.
About about 15 minutes later...
I went back but you were gone.
I promise.
I promise.
I promise I went back.

ASHA- Pull a scarf round my neck.
Cold out.

NID- Cold.

ASHA- It's cold.

NID- Pull a jacket round my shoulders.
Going out.
Going out to –
Yeah.
Finally.
Finally.

ASHA- Brush my hair.
Teeth.

NID- Mascara.
Pinch my cheeks.

They practice

ASHA- Hello.

NID- Hello.

ASHA- Hi.

NID- Hi.

ASHA- Nice to meet you.

NID- It's lovely to meet you.

Back to present

ASHA- Heels, not too high.

NID- Blouse not too open - I'm a mother.

ASHA- Nails – red.

NID- Nails – red.

ASHA- And I /paint my face.
10 9 8 7 6 5 4 3 2

NID- And I paint my face.
10 9 8 7 6 5 4 3 2

ASHA- Standin' in front of Boots. I picked it. Thought, you know, somewhere public, in case, in case anythin'...
It's rainin'.
I didn't bring an umbrella.
I pull my hood up.
Hope I don't look...

NID- Standing opposite the Boots now, standing where we said. Quite a crowd. Maybe not the best... anyway.
Chips on my nails already.
I baked her a birthday cake, just a gesture.
I can see the time in an office block window. I'm early. I'm early and I've been here 10 minutes. I couldn't. I couldn't waste any more time. How'll I know her when I see her?

ASHA- Put a flower in my hair. You know like in the films, 'I'll be the one with the flower in my hair...'

NID- 4 minutes.
There's a girl.
About 5ft 6. Looks, could be Italian, could be Spanish, could be half of me. I don't know, she's got her hood

up, she's crouching into the wall, trying to shelter from the rain.

ASHA- There's a girl, woman. Red nails. Box in her hands. She's white.
She catches my eye.

NID- She catches my eye.

ASHA- Is that –

NID- Her?

ASHA- She's on the wrong side. It's not.

NID- Maybe she meant to meet... no.

ASHA- Doesn't even look like me.

NID- 2 minutes.

ASHA- I mean maybe.

NID- She's still looking at me. Looking, looking away.

BEAT

NID- Step, take a step.

ASHA- She's stepped out, she's comin', she's, is –

NID- See the lights change from green to amber to red.

ASHA- I want to run to her but my feet are stuck.

NID- Cars slow to a stop.

ASHA- Steps out into the road.

NID- She's looking at me.

ASHA- She's lookin' at me.
She doesn't look like me.

NID- She has her father's eyes.

ASHA- BANG
No no no no
Slow
It all moves slow.
Slow
Watchin'
So slow
Helpless to stop
See it comin' see it comin' why didn't you see it comin'.
On the road. Body on the road. Body like mine. Body like my body. Body under the wheels of a van. People yellin', people screamin'.

Hello? Hello? Please, there's been an accident,
there's been, my mother, my mum –
Cold.

NID- Cold.

ASHA- Pull a scarf round my neck.
Cold out.

NID- Pull a jacket round my shoulders.
Going out.
Going out to –
Yeah.
Finally.
Finally.

ASHA- Brush my hair.
Teeth.

NID- Mascara.
Pinch my cheeks.

They practice

ASHA- Hello.

NID- Hello.

ASHA- Hi.

NID- Hi.

ASHA- Nice to meet you.

NID- It's lovely to meet you.

Back to present

ASHA- Heels, not too high.

NID- Blouse not too open - I'm a mother.

ASHA- Nails – red.

NID- Nails – red.

ASHA- And I paint my face.
10 9 8 7 6 5 4 3 2

NID- And I paint my face.
10 9 8 7 6 5 4 3 2
.

Standing opposite the Boots now, standing where we said. Quite a crowd. Maybe not the best… anyway. Chips on my nails already.
I baked her a birthday cake, just a gesture.
I can see the time in an office block window. I'm early. I'm early and I've been here 10 minutes. I couldn't. I couldn't waste any more time. How'll I know her when I see her?

ASHA- Standin' in front of Boots. I picked it. Thought, you know, somewhere public, in case, in case anythin'...
It's rainin', I didn't bring an umbrella, I pull my hood up, hope I don't look...

NID- 4 minutes.

ASHA- Put a flower in my hair. You know like in the films, 'I'll be the one with the flower in my hair...'

NID- There's a girl.
About 5ft 6. Looks, could be Italian, could be Spanish, could be half of me. I don't know, she's got her hood up.
She's crouching into the wall, trying to shelter from the rain.

ASHA- There's a girl, woman. Red nails. Box in her hands. She's Asian.

NID- She catches my eye.

ASHA- She catches my eye.

NID- Asha?

ASHA- Is that —

NID- I –

ASHA- She's on the wrong side. It's not.

NID- Maybe she meant to meet… no.

ASHA- Doesn't even look like me.

NID- 2 minutes.

ASHA- I mean maybe.

NID- She's still looking at me. Looking, looking away.

ASHA- Step, take a step.

NID- She's stepped out, she's coming she's, is –

ASHA- Watch the lights change from green to amber to red.

NID- I want to run away but my feet are stuck.

ASHA- Cars pull to a stop.

NID- 30 seconds.

ASHA- I step out into the road.

NID- 20.

ASHA- She's lookin' at me.

NID- She's looking at me.
Want to look away.
She doesn't look like me.

ASHA- Nothin' like me.

NID- BANG
On the road. Body on the road. Body like mine. Body like my body should be my body. Body not a body, not anything, not anyone, nothing any more. Flesh sinking into the bonnet of a car. People yelling, people screaming.
Hello? Hello? Please, there's been an accident, there's been, my daughter, my daughter –

PAUSE

NID- That is why I have no daughter.

ASHA- That's why I have no mother.

NID- /No other reason.

ASHA- No other reason. None.

NID- None.

PAUSE

NID- I'm 102 years young.

Ashes – that's what I always wanted.

Nice for us all. Good way to say good bye I think.

2 stand on the edge - Saj's arm around Sara.

Sara turns into her Papa Bear's body and then her fingers gentle, gently lift all that's left of me, lift –

Let go.

Let go.

Let me go girl.

Wind catches me –

FREE.

Slipping through fingers like silk.

6pm.

ASHA- I'm 81. 6pm.

Skin drippin' off my bones, loose like sheets hangin' from the line. Small bones but hard.

A 5 foot box.

Arms folded over my chest. White blouse. Odd angle - my head. Such an odd -

Look away. Fast. No more. Fast. Over. Done. Only a body. Mine. Only skin. Just –

Close the casket.

Lower me slow.

Bury me deep.

NID- I'm 92. 7pm

If you don't have anyone to throw them, what do
they do with the ashes?
No Adnan, no mum, no dad, no love nor daughter.
Not a thing left. All gone. Maybe there's a grandchild
- little part of me, her. I wouldn't know... but I'd like
that.

ASHA- I'm 71 years old.
Is it possible d'you think, that pieces of me are still,
could still be floatin' around inside of her?
She's.
Probably dead she is.
Maybe, dunno.
It's 7pm.

NID- 82, I'm 82.
I run my hand along my knee. Leather knee. Leather
elephant knee.
I look in the mirror, pull back my hair and hold it up
tight. The line of my jaw so like my father's now sags.
Deep rich brown of my skin losing its shine. Smoke
black hair now white. I see the colours, the defining
features, all that I thought were me, were strong and
bold and us – all dissolvin', melting like butter.
8pm.

ASHA- I'm 61. 8pm.
She's.
Probably dead she is.
Maybe, dunno.

Never got to meet her granddaughter, nah.
Could be 89, could be 101, could be 93, 94, 95 – she
could be any of the numbers.
Dunno.
Better -

NID- 9pm, I'm 72.
Don't expect it, not now, no.
Trying to just –

ASHA- Drown.
Drown in my bath.
HIV positive. I'm positive.
Virus won't take me. Rather me take me, now, when
I'm still capable. When the inside ain't yet visible on
the out.
Can drown in an inch of water. Ever hear that? It's
true.
Not sure if I'm drownin' or becomin' the water.
Water and me. We're the same. Same colour. I'm
dissolvin' into it. Floatin' on its surface now. Skin o'
me, skin o' it. And it's good, it's nice - being a part of
something.
I'm 51, it's 9p.m.

NID- 62 years old, 10p.m.
I don't work anymore.
Just waste time growing flowers in the garden.
Waste time pressing flowers between books. Waste

time noting time - writing birthday cards, going to funerals, weddings.
Waiting – seems like just waiting.

ASHA- I'm 41.
I work in a shop. Clothes. Well, fabric, rolls of fabric... silks and linen. Beautiful colours, just rolling sheets between my fingers all day long. Been a long day, checking the stocking, then –
2 men.
I - We're closed.
Balaclavas.
I see... Fuck off! Get out! Get -
2 men in balaclavas – the last faces I ever see, but I never really got to see their faces. He, the taller one, he calls me, "beautiful, beautiful", these are the last words I ever hear and the first time I've ever heard them.
Thank you.
10p.m.

NID- I'm 52, 11p.m.
There's a man I see him on the bus.
Tall man.
Sharp cheek bones and shaved head.
Deeply inset eyes.
I imagine him taking her to his bed.
Imagine him taking her, pushing and pulling and -

ASHA- At 11pm. At 31.

I haven't bled in 3 years.

NID- I'm 42.
She's…
Probably dead she is.
Maybe, don't know…
Could be 21. Dead or 21. Either. One or the other.
I don't know.
People, people, newspapers, bags, trains, clock -
clock on the wall both hands so so close to the 12.

ASHA- 11:58p.m. I'm 21, 21 at midnight.
I was born.
21 years ago - I know that I was born, I know that.
But I dunno the land, dunno the body I came from.
Will I know it when I see it?
Feel it when I'm there?
I worry it doesn't even exist.
Cause if I'm from here and there. If I'm from a him
and a her then there is no one place. Is there? There
is no common ground. Can't split myself in two.
I've tried.
Pull out my nose and hurl it over there?
Rip out my eyebrows drop 'em here?
Separate the speckles of green from the brown mist
in my eyes but –
Can't. I can't.

NID- I'm 42.
She's 21. She is 21 at midnight.

11:59p.m.
The big hand will pound forward.

ASHA- 59

NID- Too late now.

ASHA- 58

NID- At 11:59 on 1st July I feel the train coming.
See the train coming.
She's -

ASHA- 57.

NID- Probably dead she is.
Maybe, dunno.
Can't give a kid up 21 years ago and ask for
forgiveness now.

ASHA- 56
55.
Find me?

NID- She would have found me if she'd wanted to.

ASHA- 54.
Never too late.

NID- Too late now.

Just have to live with it now.

ASHA counts as NID speaks, she gets stuck on 2

ASHA- 53, 52, 51, 50, 49, 48, etc...7, 6, 5, 4, 3, 3, 4, 2, 2

NID- /Live with it or die with it...
I'm sorry, I'm sorry you weren't born to someone else.
Too good for me, you were always too good for me.
I haven't been here for 21 years.
For 21 years a Londoner bypasses King's Cross Station. The taxis I've taken, the long routes round, the extra half hour on a bus... all to avoid this – all to forget you.
And now, here I am.
Breathing in dirt and dust and heat.
Trains rumbling past.
There are a few free seats on the platform, but I don't want to sit. I want to stand and move and... do, do something, for once – do something Nid.
I close my eyes, inhale and exhale slowly, letting the air whistle past my lips, tasting each molecule.
I can feel you.
We're breathing the same air, this same air circulating for 21 years.
I take a step towards the yellow line and look at the thick heavy paint dividing danger from safe.

Could, could pieces of you still be floating around inside of me?

I wrap my arms around my stomach – hold you in, close and hug you tight.

I take a step – I stand on the yellow line, look down and see tiny mice scamper between the tracks.

The air is growing warmer, it's getting all warm Ash, warm, warm, scared, comforted – a web.

Orange words flash on the board and sentences stream out over the tannoy.

I step and cross the yellow line, lean my toes over the edge.

Look down and there's a whole ocean and all I want is to tumble and wade with you through the blue.

A sudden rush of air and the waves tunnel towards us.

You cling to my leg but you're smiling.

The ground under our feet begins to hum.

You reach up to me and I take your hand.

Warm air on our legs and arms, warm air blowing the hair from our eyes.

You're giggling, swinging my arm up and down and up and down.

I look into your eyes and I – you have the most beautiful eyes my baba.

You – stick out your tongue and wrinkle up your nose.

Then you – 3.

We count.

I – 3.

You – 2.

I – 2.

We're rocking back on our heels.

We're looking into one another's eyes then looking into the depths before us.

We're bending our knees, holding our joined hands up to the sky.

I – I love you.

You – I love you.

We – I love you.

Scream, cry, suck the air in.

Look at the clock – midnight.

My last everything.

I will remember you.

And together we –

NID's mobile rings.
She listens to it for some time then takes some calming deep breathes before wiping her face and answering.

NID- Hello, hello sweetheart, what are you doing up so late huh, shouldn't you be in bed-

For me? I don't... you shouldn't wait for me... I'm just... yes... soon, soon ok, of course, of course, of course I'll read you a story. Yeah, the one with the bear. I'll be home soon. Ok, you just –

Yes, yes, I promise. I promise I won't be long, I promise I won't be long.

NID takes a step backwards - away from the tracks

NID- See you soon, sweetheart can, can you put your Dad on the phone. K, bye, k...
Saj Saj –

ASHA- 2.

NID- I have two-

ASHA- 2

NID- I have two-
.
I have two daughters.
....

RAY sleeps.
ASHA is beside him, wide awake, looking at him.

ASHA- 1.
.
I love you.

PAUSE

RAY moves slightly and ASHA closes her eyes tight.

BEAT

ASHA slowly reopens her eyes.

BEAT

*RAY moves, ASHA closes her eyes and turns away
from Ray.*
ASHA opens her eyes, she still faces away from Ray.

SILENCE

An alarm sounds.

ASHA remains still.
RAY turns the alarm off and gets up.
He begins to dress.
ASHA continues to face away.

RAY picks up his keys.

*ASHA gets out of bed, never looking at RAY's face,
she kisses him.*
She pulls his t-shirt off.
He stops.

.

Looks at her.

.

*RAY tries to put his t-shirt back on but ASHA keeps
hold of it. She looks him right in the face.*

RAY tries to take his t-shirt

ASHA keeps hold of it.

SILENCE

ASHA lets go of the t-shirt.

ASHA- Go.

RAY pulls his t-shirt on and moves to exit.
He opens the door (his back to ASHA), moves to exit.

ASHA- Kissed him.

BEAT

ASHA- I kissed him.

RAY- Was more than a kiss.

ASHA- No.

RAY- No?

ASHA- No, didn't mean anythin', don't know why you're makin' such a big deal /outta –

RAY- Almost.

ASHA- What?

RAY- Almost believed you.

ASHA- True. /Truth.

RAY- Gettin' real good at it.

ASHA- /Not -

RAY- Almost managed to convince yourself.

ASHA- Fuck off.

RAY- One more time.
.
Last time.

BEAT

ASHA- Fuck. Off.

RAY exits, the door closing behind him.

SILENCE

ASHA alone.
ASHA gets into bed.

SILENCE

ASHA stands.

ASHA makes the bed.
ASHA sits on the side of the bed.

SILENCE

ASHA moves to the door.
She does not open the door, instead she speaks to it/through it.

ASHA- I'm sorry.

BEAT

ASHA- I'm sorry.

SILENCE

ASHA- I want to come.

SILENCE

ASHA- I want to go to your home and meet them. I want to but I'm afraid. I am so afraid that they will meet me and they will not like me and then you'll leave me.
You will, you'll leave me.
And that is terrifyin', that's...
That's all.

SILENCE

ASHA moves back to the bed.
The door handle turns but the door is locked.

A knock on the door.

ASHA- Hello?

RAY- It's me.

ASHA- Did you forget something?

ASHA unlocks the door - lets RAY in.

RAY- I love you too.

ASHA- ...

RAY- Come to dinner tonight, 7:30.

RAY kisses ASHA on the cheek.
ASHA is silent.

RAY- 7:30.

RAY exits

ASHA is alone.

SILENCE

NID- I'm 42.
You're 21. It's your birthday Ash, wake up, it's your birthday. 21! Keys to the house.
(*sings*) Happy Birthday to you.
Happy Birthday to you.
Happy Birthday dear Asha.
Happy Birthday to you.

PAUSE

ASHA dials.

ASHA- 7:30, I'll be there, I'll bring cake.

End.